Helping Children See Jesus

ISBN: 978-1-933206-21-9

JUSTIFICATION
New Testament Volume 20
Romans Part 2

Author: Marilyn P. Habecker
Illustrator: Frances H. Hertzler
Colorization courtesy of Good Life Ministries
Typesetting and Layout: Morgan Melton, Patricia Pope

© 2018 Bible Visuals International
PO Box 153, Akron, PA 17501-0153
Phone: (717) 859-1131
www.biblevisuals.org

All rights reserved. No part of this publication may be reproduced, stored in a retrieval system or transmitted in any form by any means, electronic, mechanical, photocopy, recording or otherwise, without the prior permission of the publisher, except as provided by USA copyright law.

RELATED ITEMS

To access related items (such as activities, memory verse posters and translated texts) please visit our web store at www.biblevisuals.org and enter 1000 at the top right of the web page. You may need to reduce the zoom setting to get the search box.

FREE TEXT DOWNLOAD

To obtain a FREE printable copy of the English teaching text (PDF format) under Product Format, please scroll down and select Extra–PDF Teacher Text Download. Then under Language select English before clicking the ADD TO CART button to place in your shopping cart. Other languages are available at an additional cost from the Language menu. When checking out, use coupon code XTACSV17 at checkout and click on Apply Coupon to receive the discount on the English text.

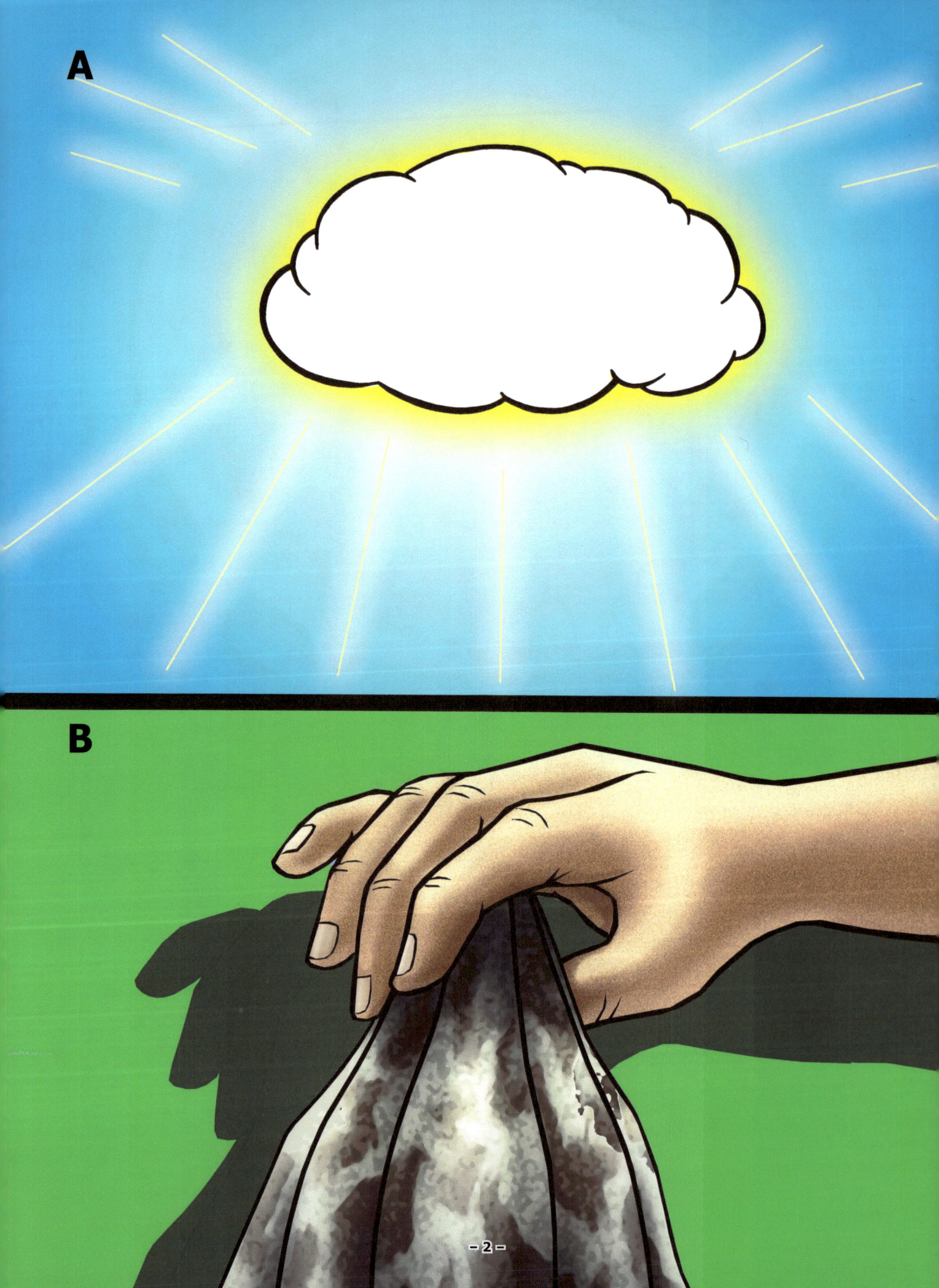

A B

C

Therefore being justified by faith, we have peace with God through our Lord Jesus Christ.

Romans 5:1

© Bible Visuals International Inc

Lesson 1
GOD, THE RIGHTEOUS ONE, JUSTIFIES

NOTE TO THE TEACHER

In this Visualized Bible series, the five volumes (Volumes 19 through 23) on Romans are really one unit. Each builds upon the other. For example, the subject of justification needs the background of the teaching on condemnation in the preceding volume.

In presenting this volume on the doctrine of justification, we need to be clear as to the meaning of the term. "Justification" means to declare righteous; to announce a right relationship. It does not mean to make righteous. As long as we walk the earth in our human bodies, we shall retain the same sinful nature. In our earthly lives we shall never be completely righteous, but as Christians we are declared righteous and accepted as though we are righteous. How can this be? Because our faith is in the Lord Jesus Christ, who died for our sins and rose again for our justification.

We suggest that you teach the memory verse at the conclusion of this lesson.

Scripture to be studied: Romans 3:9–4:25

The *aim* of the lesson: To teach the meaning of justification: God declares Christian believers righteous even though they were once guilty sinners.

What your students should *know*: God declares righteous those who have trusted in the Lord Jesus Christ.

What your students should *feel*: A desire to be declared righteous.

What your students should *do*:

Unsaved: Believe in Jesus Christ as the Son of God and accept Him as Saviour.

Saved: Thank God for providing a way for them to be declared righteous.

Lesson outline (for the teacher's and students' notebooks):

1. God condemns sinners (Romans 3:9-20).
2. God is righteous–absolutely just (Romans 3:21-26).
3. Jesus Christ took the punishment for sin (Isaiah 53:6; 1 Peter 2:24).
4. God declares believers righteous (justified) (Romans 3:22).

The verse to be memorized:

Therefore being justified by faith, we have peace with God through our Lord Jesus Christ. (Romans 5:1)

REVIEW

1. Who wrote the letter to the Romans that is in our Bible? *(Paul)*
2. What sort of person was Paul before he became a Christian? *(He was zealous and self-righteous, thinking he was pleasing God by persecuting Christians–even having them put to death.)*
3. How did he become a Christian? *(Let someone tell of his conversion on the road to Damascus.)*
4. How was he changed? *(See Romans 1:16.)*
5. What is the theme of the book of Romans? *(The righteousness of God)*

THE LESSON
1. GOD CONDEMNS SINNERS
Romans 3:9-20

In his letter to the Romans (1:18–3:20), the Apostle Paul told the believers that sinners are condemned by God.

Show Illustration #1A

Because God is holy and perfect, He cannot approve sin. The whole world stands before Him, the Judge of all the earth. And He, the righteous One, declares that sinners are guilty and sentences them to punishment. They are condemned.

Show Illustration #1B

How did God punish His favored people, the Jews, when, instead of worshiping Him, they worshiped the golden calf? *(Three thousand men were killed in one day.)*

Show Illustration #1C

How did He punish the wicked city of Sodom? *(He rained hot melted stone and fire upon it–killing every person, each growing thing, and destroying the entire area completely.)* What an example of the awful consequences of sin!

Show Illustration #1D

God spared the city of Nineveh, even after He had said He would destroy it. Why? (Allow class to review the story of the repentance of the Ninevites, emphasizing their turning to God from sin.)

Paul says in Romans that we, too, are guilty sinners who deserve God's punishment. All of us–whether young or old, rich or poor, kind or unkind, important or unknown–have sinned. God has a perfect standard and no one has measured up to it. We miss the mark of God's perfect standard. And that is sin. (See Romans 3:23.) Nothing that we ourselves can do will make us good enough to be accepted by God. He says, "There is none righteous, no, not one . . . There is none that seeks after God . . . There is none that does good, no, not one." (See Romans 3:10-12.) And because all people everywhere are sinners, they are condemned–condemned by God Himself. This we learn from the opening chapters of Romans (1:18-3:20).

2. GOD IS RIGHTEOUS– ABSOLUTELY JUST
Romans 3:21-26

However, that is not the end. Even though all are sinful and unrighteous, we read: "But now the righteousness of God is made known" (Romans 3:21). And this is what the book of Romans is all about: *The righteousness of God.*

What does "the righteousness of God" mean? At least two things:

– 18 –

Show Illustration #2A

(1) It means that *God is always right*. He is perfect. He is holy. He is pure. He is good. He has no sin. He cannot do wrong. (*Teacher:* At the top of the illustration, print the word *Righteousness*. Inside the glory cloud print *God*. In the rays coming from the cloud, print the words that appear in the paragraph above: Right, Perfect, Holy, Pure, Good, No sin, No wrong.)

Unbelievers are the exact opposite of God. They are *not* righteous (Romans 3:10). They do not do good (Romans 3:11). They have sinned (Romans 3:23). They cannot do right (Romans 3:9-18). They fall short of the perfect standard of God (Romans 3:23). So God says that even the very best things they can do–all their righteousnesses–are like "filthy rags." (See Isaiah 64:6.)

Show Illustration #2B

(*Teacher:* Print at bottom of illustration: *Righteousness of unbelievers = filthy rags*.)

Because God is perfect goodness, He cannot approve sin. He cannot let "filthy rags" come near Him. So He must do something about the sin problem. And that leads us to the other meaning of righteousness.

(2) "The righteousness of God" means that God is *absolutely just*. Because He hates sin, He says that sin must be punished. How many people deserve punishment for sin? All–for all have sinned. And the punishment for sin is death. ("The soul that sinneth, it shall die"–Ezekiel 18:4; "The wages of sin is death"–Romans 6:23.) God's justice demands the death penalty. His love, however, provides a Substitute.

3. JESUS CHRIST TOOK THE PUNISHMENT FOR SIN
Isaiah 53:6; 1 Peter 2:24

So ever since time began, God has provided something or Someone to take the death punishment for the sinner.

Show Illustration #3A

The very first people who lived on this earth, Adam and Eve, disobeyed God. Disobedience is sin. And their sin had to be punished. So God took one of the very animals which Adam had named (Genesis 2:19), killed it, and used its skin to make coats for Adam and Eve. Imagine that! One of Adam's animals died so Adam and his wife could again walk and talk with God.

Show Illustration #3B

Later–and for hundreds of years–each sinner had to offer many perfect animals (or birds) to God as sacrifices for sins. There is no way of counting the thousands of animals that died, taking the death punishment for their sinful owners.

Show Illustration #3C

Then the Lord Jesus Christ came to earth. He is holy and perfect and good as God is holy and perfect and good. The Lord Jesus never sinned. But one day God placed on Him the sin of us all. (See Isaiah 53:6.) Because He, the perfect Lamb of God, took the punishment for all sin (see 1 Peter 2:24; Romans 5:6-8), the sinner who trusts in Him will not be punished. And that must be remembered! Only those who have believed in the Lord Jesus Christ and trusted in Him are saved from the eternal death punishment of sin. (See Acts 10:43.) Because God, the righteous One, is just, He has had One–His own Son–take the punishment for all. (See 2 Corinthians 5:14-15, 21.)

4. GOD DECLARES BELIEVERS RIGHTEOUS (JUSTIFIED)
Romans 3:22

But God does even more for the believer in Christ. In addition to freeing him from the punishment of sin, God declares the believer "righteous." Before he trusted in the Lord Jesus, that person's righteous acts were "filthy rags" in God's sight. Now, because of his faith in God's Son, the believer is declared righteous. How can this be?

In His own wonderful way, God sees each one who believes in His Son, just as He sees His Son–righteous.

Show Illustration #4

God gave Adam and Eve animal skins as coverings for their sins. But He gives a "robe of righteousness" (see Isaiah 61:10; also Job 29:14; Isaiah 11:5; 59:17; Romans 3:22; Revelation 19:8) to everyone who has trusted in His Son. He sees each one covered by the precious blood of the Lord Jesus Christ and declares him righteous. Why? Because Christ the Holy One took the guilty sinner's place and paid the death penalty.

This act of God's declaring righteous those once guilty sinners who have trusted in His Son, is known as "Justification." And that is the subject of our study in this volume.

Will you please write in your notebook the title:

Justification

"Justify" means *to declare righteous*. God says to the person who trusts in His Son, "You are justified." The holy, righteous God declares righteous those who trust in His righteous Son. Also, please write the memory verse–Romans 5:1.

Our memory verse says several things about those of us who have placed our trust in Christ.

(1) *We are justified*. We are declared righteous, which means we are in right standing with God. Who justifies? God Himself. He, the righteous One, declares us righteous.

(2) We are justified *by faith*. Does this mean that God declares everyone righteous? Oh, no! Only those who have trusted in the Son of God are justified. Before our salvation, God saw all our righteous acts as filthy rags. After our salvation, God sees us in robes of righteousness, for we are covered by His righteous Son.

(3) Being justified by faith, *we have peace with God*. Before we trusted in Christ, our sin separated us from God. We were at war with God. When two tribes are at war, there is no peace. If peace is made, there is no war. So it is with us. When we place our trust in the Son of God, the war is over. We have peace with God–peace made by God Himself.

(4) Being justified by faith, we have peace with God through our Lord Jesus Christ. The Lord Jesus has made all this possible. He died in our place. And because of what He has done God has forgiven our sins and freed us from the punishment of sin–everlasting separation from God. But He does much more: He, the righteous One, declares that we are righteous. We are justified in His sight. Have you thanked Him for that?

Lesson 2
ABRAHAM JUSTIFIED BY FAITH

> **NOTE TO THE TEACHER**
>
> The New Testament was originally written in Greek. We are indeed thankful for the scholars who laboriously translated the Bible into our language! Occasionally the translators used different words for the same Greek word. For example, in English they have used the words *righteousness* and *justification* for the same Greek root word. It is quite all right for them to have done this, for the meanings are the same. However, if you are teaching in English, you will have to make it perfectly clear that the words are interchangeable. For your sake, we trust that in your language the same word is always used.
>
> It is a tremendous thing that God, the righteous One, declares righteous those who have trusted in His Son. Let the wonder of this grip you. At the same time, remember at what great cost the Lord Jesus purchased our justification. Marvelous grace of our loving Lord!

Scripture to be studied: Romans 4; Genesis 11:31–13:18; 15:1-7; 17:1-20; 21:1-8; Nehemiah 9:7-8; Galatians 3:6; Hebrews 11:11-12

The *aim* of the lesson: To show that those who are declared righteous should live righteously.

What your students should *know*: The Lord Jesus died and rose again for their justification.

What your students should *feel*: A desire to live a righteous life.

What your students should *do*: Ask the Lord to help them live righteously. (Let each one decide upon something he can do today or tomorrow which will demonstrate his love for the Lord.)

Lesson outline (for the teacher's and students' notebooks):
1. Those who have trusted in Christ are in the family of God (John 10:28-29).
2. Abraham trusted God (Genesis 15:6; Galatians 3:6a).
3. God declares Abraham righteous (Galatians 3:6b).
4. Because Christ rose from the dead, those who trust in Him are justified (Romans 4:24-25).

The verse to be memorized:

Therefore being justified by faith, we have peace with God through our Lord Jesus Christ. (Romans 5:1)

REVIEW

1. What does "the righteousness of God" mean? *(That God is always right and that He is absolutely just)*
2. How do we know that God is always right? *(He is perfect, holy, pure, good; He has no sin; He cannot do wrong.)*
3. How many people have sinned? *(All.)*
4. Because God is just, He says that sin must be punished. What is His punishment for sin? *(Eternal death–separation from Him forever)*
5. Who were the first persons to sin? *(Adam and Eve)*
6. What did God do for Adam and Eve so that they could again walk and talk with Him? *(He killed an animal so they could have skins for coverings.)*
7. Why did the Lord Jesus die? *(To take the punishment for our sins and the sins of all the world)*
8. When we have trusted in the Lord as our Saviour, our sins are forgiven. *God took away the punishment* that we deserved. But God does more–He declares that we are . . . what? *(Righteous or Justified. He has wiped away the whole record of our sins.)*
9. What does it mean to be declared righteous? *(We are in right standing with God.)*
10. What is the theme of the book of Romans? *(The righteousness of God)*

THE LESSON

In the first part of the book of Romans (1:18-3:20), we learn that God, the righteous One, condemns sinners. But He does not want one person anywhere to be condemned. (See Matthew 18:14; 2 Peter 3:9.) So, because He is right and just, He has given His Son to take the punishment for the sins of the world. Those who trust in Him, the Lord Jesus Christ, are not condemned.

It is glorious to know and to say, "I am not condemned." But God does much more than free us of condemnation. He justifies us. God says to the person who trusts in His Son, "You are justified." Think of that! The holy, righteous God declares righteous those who believe in His righteous Son.

1. THOSE WHO HAVE TRUSTED IN CHRIST ARE IN THE FAMILY OF GOD
John 10:28-29

Show Illustration #5

Those who have received the Lord Jesus are His possession. They are in the family of God. They are held by Him. (See John 10:28-29.) Their sins (which once separated them from God) are forgiven. They are freed from eternal condemnation. And they are declared righteous by God Himself. (See Romans 8:1.) Because believers are in Christ, they are in right standing with God. They are justified.

2. ABRAHAM TRUSTED GOD
Genesis 15:6; Galatians 3:6a

To understand the meaning of justification, we turn to the book of Romans (3:21–5:21). Here God speaks of Abraham, who lived many hundreds of years before the Lord Jesus was on earth. He was the first of the Jews and became known as "Father Abraham." Abraham loved God. But he lived among people who worshiped idols. (See Joshua 24:2-3.) When Abraham was 75 years old, God said to him, "Leave your relatives and your country and go to a new land which I will show you. You will be the beginning of a great nation. I will bless you and make your name great."

Abraham did not ask God any questions. He did not say, "Why must I leave my country?" or "Where is this new country?" He did not even say, "I am too old to begin a new life in a strange place." Abraham believed that God knew what was best for him. And he trusted God to take care of him. So he packed all his belongings, took his wife, his nephew (Lot), and his servants, and began his journey, obeying God's command.

Show Illustration #6

When Abraham got to the place which God had chosen for him, God made a promise: "Look around you, Abraham," He said. "I am going to give this land to your children and your grandchildren, and to all those who will be born into your family in the years to come. Look at the stars in the sky. Can you count them? No? Neither can you count the number of children you will have."

This was a special promise indeed! But it was also very puzzling. For, you see, Abraham and his wife, Sarah, had no children. They were already getting old. Do you think that Abraham doubted God's promise? Did he say, "How can my children own this land when I do not have any children?" No. God has recorded in His Word, so that all may know: "Abraham believed in the Lord. And He counted it to him for righteousness" (Genesis 15:6). God knew what was in Abraham's heart. He knew Abraham trusted in Him. And God, the righteous One, declared Abraham righteous.

3. GOD DECLARES ABRAHAM RIGHTEOUS
Galatians 3:6b

Years passed and Abraham grew older. He had many adventures in his new homeland. Because God blessed him, Abraham became rich. But the one promise–the special one–was not yet fulfilled.

God talked with Abraham. This time He promised: "Sarah, your wife, will have a son." Abraham was delighted, though this time he asked more about it. For Sarah was already 90 years old. (See Genesis 17:17.) But God assured him, saying, "Sarah will indeed have a son, and you will call his name Isaac."

Show Illustration #7

What a glad day it was when that baby boy was born to Sarah and Abraham. Abraham had believed in the Lord. So God declared him righteous and blessed him. And his children, the Jews, are all over the world even today–hundreds of years since Isaac was born.

Why did God declare Abraham righteous? Was it because Abraham did good works? Was it because Abraham went through a religious ceremony (circumcision)? Was it because Abraham obeyed the Jewish Law? No. Because Abraham's trust was in God, God declared him righteous.

4. BECAUSE CHRIST ROSE FROM THE DEAD, THOSE WHO TRUST IN HIM ARE JUSTIFIED
Romans 4:24-25

And so it is with us. We are not declared righteous because of our good works. We are not declared righteous by performing religious acts. We are not declared righteous by obeying laws. We can never do anything that would cause God to declare us righteous. How then can we be declared righteous? How can we be justified? By placing our trust in God's Son.

The very last verse of the fourth chapter of Romans gives us the clue as to how God can righteously declare believers righteous. There we read that the Lord Jesus died for our sins and *was raised again for our justification.*

Show Illustration #8

It was because of our sins that Christ died. (See 2 Corinthians 5:21.) His blood paid the price for our sins. (See Romans 5:9.) His resurrection is proof that God is satisfied with that price. And because God is satisfied with what the Lord Jesus did, He declares righteous those who trust in Him.

Suppose we allow this little stone to represent me. (*Teacher:* Use any small object.) What is this stone's name? (Your pupils should answer with your name, teacher.) Here is a cross. (You can cut or tear it out of paper or cloth or a banana leaf–whatever is available.) Who died on the cross? The Lord Jesus Christ. One day I believed that Jesus is the Son of God. I knew that I was a sinner and that my sins would separate me from God forever. But I learned that the Lord Jesus died on the cross, taking my sins upon Himself. I placed my trust in Him–recognizing Him as my Substitute. I received Him as my very own Saviour. Since that moment I have been "in Christ." (*Teacher:* Wrap stone in cross.) Now, when God looks at me, He sees where I am. Where is that? In Christ. (See Romans 8:1; 1 Corinthians 1:30; 2 Corinthians 5:17; Philippians 1:1; Colossians 1:2; 1 Thessalonians 4:16.)

So God sees me through His Son, the righteous One. And He declares me righteous. I am justified.

Does that mean I am perfect and sinless? You all know me. Do you honestly think that ever since I was born into the family of God I have been without sin? I'm sure you don't. Altogether too often I have failed. God knows me even better than you know me. He knows the wrong things that I do, and He also knows the wrong thoughts I have; He knows my wrong motives. But because I am in His Son, He declares me righteous.

This is a very serious thing. It fills me with shame when I think of what my sins cost the Saviour. But, remembering what He did for me, I want to live a righteous life. With all my heart I want to prove by my daily life that I am justified.

What about you? If you are already in Christ, would you this moment ask the Lord to help you to live righteously as proof to others that you have been declared righteous by God? (*Teacher:* Let your class discuss how their lives should be different from those who have not received Christ as Lord and Saviour.)

Lesson 3
HOW GOD JUSTIFIES (IMPUTATION)

Scripture to be studied: Romans 4:3-6, 8-11, 22-24; 5:12-21; Philemon

The *aim* of the lesson: To teach the meaning of imputation: to put to the account of another.

What your students should *know*: God puts His righteousness to the account of everyone who believes in Christ.

What your students should *feel*: Thankful that God imputes His righteousness to those who receive Christ.

What your students should *do*:

Unsaved: Believe in the Lord Jesus Christ as the Son of God and receive Him as Saviour.

Saved: Thank God for imputing His righteousness to them. Determine something good they can do today proving their love for the Lord Jesus.

Lesson outline (for the teacher's and students' notebooks):

1. The sin of Adam is imputed to all who have been born since Adam (Romans 5:12-14).
2. Onesimus, a slave, sins (Philemon 15-18).
3. Onesimus turns to Christ and returns to his master (Philemon 10-13).
4. Because sin was imputed to Christ, the righteousness of God is imputed to all who trust in Christ (Romans 5:15-21).

The verse to be memorized:

Therefore being justified by faith, we have peace with God through our Lord Jesus Christ. (Romans 5:1)

> ### NOTE TO THE TEACHER
> In order to understand how God, the righteous One, can justify guilty sinners who trust in His Son, we have to learn another Bible word: Imputation. The Greek word logizomai is translated by three different English words: count, reckon, and impute. All of these appear in the fourth chapter of Romans, as indicated above in the Scripture to be studied. Though different words are used, all have the same meaning: *to put to one's account.* (If you are working in a language other than English, you will want to check the verses to see if the same word is used in Romans 4 verses 3, 4, 5, 6, 8, 9, 10, 11, 22, 23 and 24, or if different words are used.)
>
> We have chosen to tell the story of Philemon since it illustrates imputation. Remember, teacher, that stories which illustrate a truth are windows that let in the light. Use such stories frequently.

THE LESSON

God justifies the believer in Christ. What does it mean to be justified? (It means to be counted righteous.) Is a person justified because he does good works? (No.) Is he justified by obeying God's law? (No.) Is he justified by performing religious ceremonies? (No.) How, then, is he justified? (By placing his trust in the Lord Jesus Christ.)

Abraham, who lived hundreds of years before Jesus came to earth, believed in the Lord. And because he believed in the Lord, we read that God "counted it to him for righteousness" (Genesis 15:6; Romans 4:3). In Romans 4:22 it says "it was imputed to him for righteousness." This is justification–God declared him righteous. But to understand *how* God justifies, we must understand the meaning of the words "counted to him" and "imputed." So today we want to study *imputation*.

Please write in your notebook the title of this lesson:

Romans 4; 5:12-21

Has anyone ever said to you, "You look just like your father"? Or, "You walk like your mother"? That is because children are often copies of their parents. The good and bad qualities of their parents are passed on to them. They "inherit" the nature of their parents.

1. THE SIN OF ADAM IS IMPUTED TO ALL WHO HAVE BEEN BORN SINCE ADAM
Romans 5:12-14

Adam and Eve were the first people on this earth. God made them so that they could choose either to obey Him or not to obey Him. Not to obey God is sin. And Adam and Eve chose not to obey God.

Show Illustration #9

Because the very first parents, Adam and Eve, were sinners, their children were sinners. Their children's children were sinners. And every person who has since come into the world has been born with a sinful heart. Why? Because we have inherited the sin nature of Adam, the first father. Every time we sin, we prove this to be true. We automatically do wrong. We have to learn to do right. No baby has to be taught to cry if he does not get his own way. No child has to be taught to lie. He does have to be taught to tell the truth. Why? Because he is like the first father: sinful.

The sin of Adam is imputed to us. Please write in your notebook the meaning of "impute":

"Impute" means *to put to one's account.* (*Teacher:* Please use a local illustration to explain the meaning of imputation. The one we use here may not be typical of your area.) Let us suppose that on market day your father needs to get some fish (or rice, or corn–or whatever your people use daily). But on that day your father does not have any money. So he goes to the man from whom he usually buys fish and says, "I want to buy some fish. But I would like you to put it on my son's account. He will pay you the money that I owe." If the fish man agrees to this, you become responsible for your father's debt. What your father owes has been put to your account. That is imputation.

In a similar way, the sin of Adam is charged to the account of each person (except Christ Jesus) who has been born since Adam. His sin is imputed to us (Romans 5:12-21). The result of his sin is also imputed to us. What is the result of Adam's sin? Death–eternal death. And eternal death is separation from God forever and forever. (See Romans 5:12, 17-19, 21.)

But God the righteous One has done a glorious thing. He placed the sin of the world on His perfect, righteous Son. (See Isaiah 53:4-6; 1 Peter 2:24.) Your sins and mine have been put to the account of the Lord Jesus Christ. By His death on the cross, He paid the debt of our sin. He, our Substitute, bore the wrath due us and settled the account of our sin once and for all.

God does even more! When our faith is in the Lord Jesus, God puts all of His righteousness to our account. Just as God imputed His righteousness to Abraham because he believed in Him, so God imputes His own righteousness to those who trust in Christ. Because God has put His righteousness to the believer's account, He can righteously declare the believer righteous. Justification is possible because of imputation–and God does it all!

2. ONESIMUS, A SLAVE, SINS
Philemon 15-18

These things we learn as we study the book of Romans. Who wrote the book of Romans? The Apostle Paul. In another of Paul's letters–the Epistle to Philemon–he wrote again about imputation. Though the word itself does not appear, the truth is there. Listen carefully and see if you can detect it.

The Bible does not give a full account of all of the events but from what it does say we believe the story that follows tells the facts as they may have happened.

Philemon (to whom Paul wrote his letter) lived in the city of Colosse. He was doubtless a rich man. One of his slaves, Onesimus, decided that he wanted his freedom. He wanted to go far away to the famous city of Rome. But how could he escape? If he ran away and got caught, he would be killed at once. For that was the punishment of a runaway slave in those days. Besides, what could he do if he did run away? He had no money. How could he get to Rome? Finally he decided upon a plan.

Show Illustration #10

One night when Philemon was asleep, Onesimus tiptoed to the place where Philemon kept his money. Onesimus slipped the moneybag under his coat and, making certain that no one heard or saw him, he sneaked out of the house. He darted noiselessly from one shadow to another. When he got to the edge of the city, he ran as fast as he could run.

He wanted to get far away while it was dark. At daylight Onesimus found a safe place to hide. There he slept.

That night, when all was again dark, he hurried on. Night after night he kept going farther away. When he got to the seashore, he found a ship that would be crossing the Aegean Sea. (*Teacher:* We are not certain what route Onesimus took. Ephesus was about 100 miles from Colosse, and from there he may have gone by ship to Greece.) When no one was looking, Onesimus hid down in the ship. It was not easy to be a stowaway but he was determined to get as far away as he could. So he rolled and tossed across the sea to Greece.

3. ONESIMUS TURNS TO CHRIST AND RETURNS TO HIS MASTER
Philemon 10-13

Show Illustration #11

He fled through Greece by night, and once again came to the seashore. Again he hid in a ship, this time crossing the Adrian Sea. After many nights, Onesimus got to Italy. Finally he was in Rome! He was safe! No one knew him there. (He was about 800 miles from Colosse.) No one could know that he was a runaway slave. He was seeing the famous city and its famous people with his very own eyes. He was free!

One day, in some unexplained way, Onesimus met a famous missionary–the Apostle Paul. And he met him in prison. Imagine that! Paul was in prison for having preached the Gospel, but even there–in prison–he kept right on preaching. The time came when the sinful Onesimus believed the Gospel message and placed his trust in the Saviour, Jesus Christ. Immediately he became helpful to Paul–so helpful, indeed, that Paul wished he could keep him in Rome. (See Philemon 11 and 13.) But Paul knew that Philemon had purchased Onesimus. And it was Onesimus's place to be in Philemon's home, serving.

When Paul told Onesimus that it was his Christian duty to return to Philemon, Onesimus was terrified. "Philemon will kill me! That's what happens to all runaway slaves!" he cried.

"If he kills you, it will be what you deserve. You knew before you ran away that your punishment could be death. But Philemon is my friend. He is a Christian. And now you are a fellow Christian. I'll write a letter for you to take to him. We can trust the Lord to do whatever is best."

Because Paul may have had eye trouble, he usually had someone else write his letters for him. This time he wrote himself. Onesimus guarded that letter carefully as he trudged those hundreds of miles back to Colosse. When he finally reached Philemon's home, terror struck him. *I can't go back! He'll kill me!* he thought. He could not make himself rap at the gate. *I've got to! I must! I'm a Christian now,* he told himself. With a prayer to God for courage, he tapped on the gate. And before he had a chance to run, Philemon was there.

"Here's a letter from Paul!" Onesimus exclaimed.

Philemon grabbed the letter and read aloud: "Paul, a prisoner for the sake of Jesus Christ, to Philemon our much-loved fellow worker . . . In my prayers I always thank God for you, Philemon . . . Although I could order you to do something which I think is right, I am not doing that. No, I am appealing to your love . . . I am appealing for Onesimus, my child in the Christian faith . . . He has been useless to you in the past. But now he is going to be useful. I am sending him back to you. Will you receive him as my son? . . . You lost him, a slave, for a time. Now you will have him back for good, not only as a slave, but as a Christian brother . . . Welcome him as you would welcome me. If he has wronged you or owes you anything, put it to my account. I have written this with my own hand. I Paul, will repay you . . . "

Think of that! Paul the missionary asked to have charged to himself the debt of Onesimus the slave. All that Onesimus owed Philemon was *imputed* to Paul. And if Philemon honored Paul's request (and we believe he did), he accepted Onesimus into his home as gladly as he would have received Paul. Onesimus's debt was put to Paul's account. And Paul's good reputation was put to Onesimus's account.

4. BECAUSE SIN WAS IMPUTED TO CHRIST, GOD's RIGHTEOUSNESS IS IMPUTED TO ALL WHO TRUST IN CHRIST
Romans 5:15-21

As wonderful as that is, God has done something far more wonderful for us.

Show Illustration #12

The Lord Jesus, by His death on the cross, has said of each sinner: "I have taken his death penalty. I am that sinner's Substitute. Put all of his sin to My account."

The moment that any sinner believes in his heart that Jesus is the Son of God and places his trust in Him, God puts to that believer's account His own righteousness. And because God's righteousness is imputed to the believer, God declares him righteous. He is justified. Is His righteousness yours? If so, have you thanked Him that this is so? If you have only your own "filthy rags" righteousness, God waits for you to receive His Son.

Lesson 4
THE RESULTS OF JUSTIFICATION

NOTE TO THE TEACHER

Many Bible scholars teach justification as the greatest and most important doctrine in the Bible. Certainly the assurance of the Christian depends on an understanding of justification.

Deuteronomy 25:1 reads, "If there is a controversy between men, and the judges have to judge them, they will justify the righteous and condemn the wicked." That is, if a man is proved innocent, he should be justified (declared righteous) before the people.

In the first three chapters of Romans we are taught that every person in the whole world stands before the Judge of all the earth. He declares they are condemned. But that is not the end. The perfect Lamb of God died on the cross and took upon Himself the sin of the world. He rose again, proving that He is the Son of God and that God is satisfied with His sacrifice. God says that when a person believes that Jesus is the Son of God and receives Him as Lord and Saviour, he is no longer condemned. Instead he is declared righteous. Why? Because God puts to the account of the believer His own righteousness. The believer receives the robe of His righteousness. That is justification. It is the free gift of God to the believer in Christ.

This is the unique message of the Gospel. The religions of the world urge people to strive to live a holy life by resolutions, by rules, by efforts, by prayers, by penance, so that God may make them worthy of Heaven. The Gospel message is exactly the opposite. God first justifies the sinner and then sets him apart, giving him the ability to live the kind of life which pleases God. (That "setting apart" by God is known as *sanctification*–which we will study in our next volume.)

Satan has deceived millions of people by causing them to believe that by being good they will earn an entrance to Heaven. May none of your pupils accept this lie of the devil! Pray that your teaching will be so clear that all will see themselves as condemned sinners. Help them to see that the Lord Jesus has already taken upon Himself their sin, paid the death penalty, and waits for them to trust in Him so that God's righteousness may be theirs.

By asking many questions, try to draw out from your class their understanding of these lessons. Be sure to get the correct answers to the questions.

Scripture to be studied: Romans 5:1-11

The *aim* of the lesson: To show what a believer receives when he is justified.

What your students should *know:* Because the Lord Jesus took the punishment for sin, all who believe in Him are declared righteous.

What your students should *feel:* Gratitude to God for imputing His righteousness to those who receive His Son.

What your students should *do:*
Saved: Examine their lives to see if they are living righteously. List in their notebooks those things they can do this week which will prove their love for Him.

Lesson outline (for the teacher's and students' notebooks):
1. Those who believe in Jesus are declared righteous (justified) (Romans 4:25; 5:9).
2. Those who are justified have peace with God and can pray to God (Romans 5:1-2).
3. Those who are justified receive a home in Heaven, the love of God and the Holy Spirit (Romans 5:2-5).
4. Justified believers have eternal life (1 Corinthians 15:22).

The verse to be memorized:

Therefore being justified by faith, we have peace with God through our Lord Jesus Christ. (Romans 5:1)

THE LESSON

1. THOSE WHO BELIEVE IN JESUS ARE DECLARED RIGHTEOUS (JUSTIFIED)
Romans 4:25; 5:9

In our last three lessons we have learned some tremendous Bible truths. What has been the subject of our study? *(Justification)* When a person is said to be justified, what does it mean? *(He has been declared righteous.)* Who declares righteous? *(God, the righteous One)*

Show Illustration #13A

(Teacher: Print the word Righteousness above the cloud, and inside the cloud print God as you did in illustration #2a.)

What does the righteousness of God mean? *(It means that God is always right. He is perfect. He is holy. He has no sin. And it also means that He is absolutely just.)* How has God proved that He is just? *(Ever since Adam and Eve sinned, He has provided something or Someone to take the death penalty which the guilty sinner deserved.)*

When Adam and Eve sinned, they made aprons of fig leaves to cover themselves. But that kind of covering was not satisfactory to God. What kind of covering did He give them? *(Coats of animal skins)* Beginning right then when the world was new, God wanted everyone to know that sin resulted in death. And He allowed the animal to be the substitute for Adam–it died in his place. In later years thousands of animals took the death penalty for sinners. (Study Hebrews 10:4.)

Then God sent His Son. He, the perfect, sinless Lamb of God died in the place of every sinner. And all who put their trust in Him are declared righteous. They are justified.

Show Illustration #13B

Because they are in Christ, even though they were guilty sinners, God declares that they are as His Son–righteous. How can God do this? What is it that justifies believers?

Show Illustration #13C

Believers are justified by the precious blood of the Lord Jesus Christ and by His resurrection. Let's read aloud together Romans 5:9 and 4:25. Does this mean that because Jesus died and rose again everyone is justified? Oh, no! Listen while I read parts of three verses from Romans 3. ". . . The righteousness of God which is by faith of Jesus Christ unto all and upon all them that *believe*." (v. 22) ". . . That He [God] might be just, and the justifier of him *which believeth in Jesus*." (v. 26) ". . . A man is justified by faith." (v. 28) What do these verses tell us? *(Those who believe in Jesus are justified.)*

2. THOSE WHO ARE JUSTIFIED HAVE PEACE WITH GOD AND CAN PRAY TO GOD
Romans 5:1-2

Have you ever received a large gift package and found when you opened it, not one gift, but many gifts? The one package contained many gifts. So it is with God's gift of justification.

In the verse we have memorized (Romans 5:1) we are told of the first gift which is part of the gift of justification. ". . . Being justified by faith, *we have peace with God* through our Lord Jesus Christ."

Show Illustration #14A

Before we trusted in the Lord Jesus Christ, we were at war with God. But the moment we believed in Him, the war was over. There was peace instead of war. And that peace is forever. In another letter Paul wrote: ". . . Having made peace through the blood of His cross . . ." (Colossians 1:20). What a price the Lord Jesus paid for us to have everlasting peace with God!

Show Illustration #14B

Another part of the justification gift is this: *we have access to God.* (See Romans 5:2a.) That is, we can pray to Him. Before the Lord Jesus came to earth, those who worshiped God were not allowed into His presence. Believers do not fear to come before God now. They know He is a loving God. And we, guilty sinners who have been justified by faith, can pray to God. Prayer is talking to Him as simply as children talk to their earthly father.

3. THOSE WHO ARE JUSTIFIED RECEIVE A HOME IN HEAVEN, THE LOVE OF GOD, AND THE HOLY SPIRIT
Romans 5:2-5

Show Illustration #15A

Because we are justified by faith in our Lord Jesus Christ, we receive another gift: a glorious *home in Heaven*. ("We rejoice in hope of the glory of God"–Romans 5:2.) Our "hope" of Heaven is sure and certain. Every believer in Christ will be forever with Him. Before getting to Heaven, however, there will be many trials (tribulation) for the Christian–trials sent by God Himself (Romans 5:3-5). If these are taken in the right way, they will make us patient, mature Christians.

Another wonderful part of the justification gift *is the love of God.* (See Romans 5:5.)

Show Illustration #15B

The love of God Himself floods the heart of the believer in Christ. Because of God's love in him, the believer does loving things for others. Our love for others is one of the proofs that we are truly justified. (See 1 John 3:14.)

We are by nature self-centered. Each one of us could carry a sign saying *Me First*. For that is the way we are. But when we allow the Holy Spirit to control our hearts, we love others, we want to do for others. We forget ourselves. Why is this so? Because God's Holy Spirit is within us.

Show Illustration #15C

Because the Holy Spirit is a Spirit, we cannot see Him. Once, at the baptism of the Lord Jesus, He did descend from Heaven in the shape of a dove. So we have used that symbol in our picture. The important truth is this: when we are justified, the Holy Spirit makes His home in our hearts (Romans 5:5b). He is included in the gift of justification.

All of this–and more–God gives to us when we are in His Son and declared righteous. And it is all free to us who believe.

But oh, what it cost the Son of God!

4. JUSTIFIED BELIEVERS HAVE ETERNAL LIFE
1 Corinthians 15:22

Show Illustration #16

The Lord Jesus Christ had been with God back in eternity past, before the world was created. Because of our sin, He humbled Himself and came to earth as a man. He, the perfect, sinless Lamb of God, was our Substitute. All of our sin was placed on Him. Why? Because ever since the first man, Adam, sinned, all have been born sinners.

Adam disobeyed God. Disobedience is sin. God condemns sinners and His punishment is death–separation from Him forever. The dark hearts on the left side of the cross remind us that people love darkness rather than light, because their deeds are evil. Those who do wrong hate the light and keep away from it, for fear their wrongs may be seen. (See John 3:19-20.)

(Teacher: On the left side of illustration #16, list the following words, please.)

Condemnation
Death

Everyone is born into Adam's family. So we, like Adam, have sinful hearts and are condemned sinners. Our punishment is eternal death.

But God, the righteous One, has given His Son to take the death punishment for the sin of the world. Obediently the Lord Jesus took upon Himself our sins and died on the cross. (See Philippians 2:8.) Because He is the Son of God, He did not stay dead. He rose and He lives. So the guilty sinner who trusts in Him has what He has.

(Teacher: On the right side of the cross, please list the words that follow.)

Righteousness
Life

Because the believer has his faith in Christ, he is declared righteous. That is because God sees him in His righteous Son. All of the righteousness of God is put to the account of the believer. So he is justified. Because the believer is in Christ, he has eternal life. "As in Adam all die, even so in Christ shall all be made alive" (1 Corinthians 15:22).

One day a man was trying to find his way through a field of dry grass that towered over his head. Suddenly he heard behind him a roaring sound. Looking back he saw huge flames of fire leaping through the dry grass toward him. He could not hope to outrun the fire. It was too hot and the strong wind was rapidly fanning the flames in his direction. What could he do?

He dropped to his knees, started another fire, and jumped back. The strong wind soon whipped this new fire into a raging blaze. The flames leaped high above his head. But the wind swiftly carried the blaze away from him leaving a wide stretch of blackened stubble. Then he stepped into the path which was *already* burned. And when the fire from behind swept toward him, it did not harm him because it could not reach him. He walked where fire had already burned. (*Teacher:* Please read Romans 5:8 to your class.)

When we have received Christ as our Saviour and are justified by His blood, we are walking where the fire of God's wrath has already burned. We are safe because Jesus has already suffered the punishment for our sin. Are you walking in this place of safety? If not, will you place your trust in the Lord Jesus right now and receive Him as your Saviour?

www.ingramcontent.com/pod-product-compliance
Lightning Source LLC
Chambersburg PA
CBHW060804090426
42736CB00002B/153